Our Favorite
Appetizer Recipes

Copyright 2015, Gooseberry Patch
Previously published under ISBN 978-1-93189-086-1
Cover: Make-Ahead Ham Bites (page 61)

A hollowed-out squash or pumpkin is a fun way to serve favorite dips...place it on a cut-glass tray and surround with a variety of crackers.

Scrumptious Bacon-Cheese Dip

Makes 7 cups

1 lb. bacon, crisply cooked
   and crumbled
2 8-oz. pkgs. shredded
   Cheddar cheese
1 onion, chopped

2 c. mayonnaise-style
   salad dressing
1/2 c. chopped pecans
assorted snack crackers

Mix together all ingredients except crackers; chill. Serve with crackers.

Nestle 2 sizes of enamelware bowls together. Fill the bottom one with crushed ice and add a fresh dip to the top bowl...keeps cold dips cool in hot weather!

Delicious Chile-Corn Dip

Makes 6 cups

3 11-oz. cans sweet corn &
    diced peppers, drained
7-oz. can chopped green chiles
6-oz. can chopped jalapeños,
    drained and liquid added
    to taste
1/2 c. green onion, chopped

1 c. mayonnaise
8-oz. container sour cream
1 t. pepper
1/2 t. garlic powder
16-oz. pkg. shredded
    sharp Cheddar cheese
scoop-style corn chips

Mix all ingredients except corn chips together and refrigerate.
Serve with corn chips.

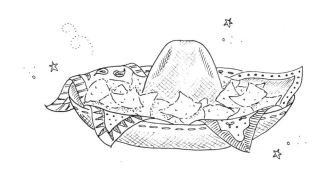

Table tents are so handy! Fold a piece of paper in half and jot down or rubber stamp the recipe name on one side. Set the table tent next to an appetizer dish so everyone will know just what's inside!

Cool & Creamy Mexican Dip *Makes 10 to 12 servings*

8-oz. pkg. cream cheese,
   softened
8-oz. container sour cream
1 c. mayonnaise
12-oz. jar salsa
1 red pepper, chopped

1 green pepper, chopped
16-oz. pkg. shredded
   Monterey Jack cheese
Optional: 3.8-oz. can sliced
   black olives, drained
tortilla chips

Combine cream cheese, sour cream and mayonnaise; spread evenly in the bottom of an ungreased 13"x9" glass baking pan. Layer remaining ingredients except tortilla chips in order listed. Chill until serving time; serve with tortilla chips.

A festive container for chips or snack mix on a party table....simply tie a knot in each corner of a brightly colored bandanna, then tuck a bowl of goodies into the center.

Homemade Guacamole

Makes about 2 cups

3 avocados, peeled, pitted
    and mashed
1/2 c. tomatoes, chopped
1/4 c. onion, chopped
2 t. garlic, minced
1 T. fresh cilantro, chopped

1 t. salt
1 t. pepper
1 t. cayenne pepper
1 t. chili powder
1/2 t. hot pepper sauce
tortilla chips

Combine ingredients except tortilla chips in order listed; mix well.
Chill; serve with tortilla chips.

Slow cookers are perfect party helpers! Just plug them in and they'll keep dips bubbly, hot and yummy with no effort at all.

Yummy Chicken-Salsa Dip

Makes 8 servings

8-oz. jar salsa, divided
8-oz. pkg. cream cheese,
   softened
8-oz. pkg. shredded
   Mexican-blend cheese

2 to 3 boneless, skinless
   chicken breasts, cooked
   and diced
tortilla chips

Blend half the salsa with the cream cheese; spread in the bottom of an ungreased 9" pie plate. Top with remaining salsa; sprinkle with cheese and chicken. Bake at 350 degrees for 25 minutes. Serve with tortilla chips.

Have a game-day appetizer buffet without the fuss.
Divide up the goodies and let guests choose one to
bring...spend less time in the kitchen and more
with family & friends!

Touchdown Hot Taco Dip

Makes 6 servings

16-oz. can refried beans
8-oz. pkg. cream cheese,
   softened
1-1/4 oz. pkg. taco
   seasoning mix

1 tomato, chopped
1/4 c. onion, chopped
1/2 c. shredded Cheddar cheese
Garnish: sour cream
corn or tortilla chips

Spread refried beans in the bottom of an ungreased 9" pie plate;
set aside. Combine cream cheese and taco seasoning; spread over
beans. Sprinkle with tomato, onion and cheese; bake at 375 degrees
for 25 to 30 minutes. Dollop with sour cream before serving; serve
with corn or tortilla chips.

Use mini cookie cutters to cut toasted bread into pleasing shapes to serve alongside savory dips and spreads.

Oh-So-Good Artichoke Dip

Makes 3 cups

28-oz. can artichokes,
   drained and chopped
1 c. mayonnaise
1 c. grated Parmesan cheese
1/8 t. garlic salt

1/8 t. Worcestershire sauce
1/8 t. hot pepper sauce
1/8 t. dill weed
Garnish: fresh parsley, chopped
toast rounds, chips or crackers

Combine artichokes, mayonnaise, cheese, garlic salt and sauces.
Spoon into a lightly greased one-quart casserole dish; sprinkle lightly
with dill. Bake at 350 degrees for 20 minutes. Garnish with parsley;
serve with toast rounds, chips or crackers.

Set herb dips or blends inside terra cotta pots
and place in a vintage carrier...ready to take to a party!

Sweet Red Pepper Dip

Makes about 3 cups

2 red peppers, halved
2 3-oz. pkgs. cream cheese,
    softened
8-oz. container sour cream

1/4 t. salt
1/4 t. paprika
1/8 t. cayenne pepper
corn or tortilla chips

Place peppers cut-side down in a microwave-safe container.
Cover and microwave on high setting for 8 to 10 minutes, or
until tender. Dip peppers into a bowl of cold water; remove skins.
Combine peppers and remaining ingredients except chips in a food
processor or blender; process until smooth. Chill for 12 hours before
serving. Serve with chips.

Bring along a tasty appetizer to the next gathering! Tuck a loaf of pumpernickel bread filled with Always-Requested Spinach Dip into a basket, surround with bread cubes and snacking crackers and deliver to your hostess...she'll love it!

Always-Requested Spinach Dip   *Makes 8 servings*

16-oz. container sour cream
1 c. mayonnaise
1-1/2 oz. pkg. onion soup
   mix, divided
4-oz. can water chestnuts,
   drained and chopped

10-oz. pkg. frozen chopped
   spinach, thawed and
   drained
16-oz. round loaf pumpernickel
   bread

Combine all ingredients except bread, using only half the package of soup mix. Save remaining mix for another recipe. Mix well; cover and refrigerate overnight. Slice off top of bread; gently tear out center, reserving bread for dipping. Spoon dip into the center of the bread; surround with reserved bread.

May our house always be too small to hold all of our friends.

-Myrtle Reed

Garden-Fresh Veggie Dip

Makes about 3 cups

1-1/3 c. sour cream
2/3 c. mayonnaise
1/4 c. fresh chives, chopped
1/4 c. onion, minced

1/4 c. pimento, chopped
1 t. garlic salt
vegetables, cut into bite-size
   pieces

Mix all ingredients together except vegetables; chill. Serve with fresh vegetables.

Create quick chip & dip sets in no time. Spoon dips into pottery soup bowls and set each bowl on a dinner plate. Surround with crackers, veggies, pretzels, chips or bread for dipping.

Seashore Crab Spread

Makes 5 to 6 cups

8-oz. pkg. cream cheese,
    softened
1 c. mayonnaise
1 c. grated Parmesan cheese
6-oz. can crabmeat, drained

14-oz. can artichokes,
    drained and chopped
1/4 c. red pepper, chopped
1/4 c. green onion, chopped
assorted snack crackers

Mix all ingredients well except crackers; spoon into an ungreased
13"x9" baking pan. Bake at 400 degrees for 20 minutes. Serve
warm with crackers.

Single servings! Roll Zippy Cheese Ball into mini balls
and place in paper muffin cups. Fill more paper muffin cups with
crackers and pretzels and arrange alongside mini cheese balls...
guests can enjoy one of each!

Zippy Cheese Ball

Makes 4 cheese balls

4 8-oz. pkgs. cream cheese,
    softened
10-oz. jar sharp pasteurized
    process cheese spread
6-oz. pkg. crumbled blue cheese

2 T. onion, grated
1 t. Worcestershire sauce
Optional: 1/2 t. flavor enhancer
8-oz. pkg. sliced almonds
assorted snack crackers

Mix all ingredients except almonds and crackers in a large bowl.
Shape into 4 balls; roll in almonds and chill. Serve with crackers.

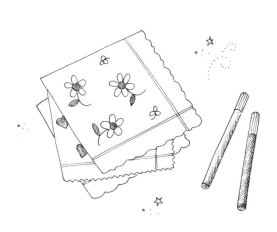

Dress up paper napkins in a snap! Trim napkin edges with decorative-edge scissors, then use permanent markers and rubber stamps to add polka dots, stripes or alphabet letters.

Dried Beef & Cheese Ball

Makes one cheese ball

2 8-oz. pkgs. cream cheese, softened
2-1/2 oz. pkg. dried beef, finely chopped
3 T. green onion, chopped
2 T. mayonnaise-style salad dressing
1 t. Worcestershire sauce
1/2 c. walnuts, chopped
round buttery crackers

Combine all ingredients except walnuts and crackers; mix well and shape into a ball. Roll in nuts and cover. Refrigerate for 3 to 4 hours before serving. Serve with crackers.

Fill baskets with dippers like pretzels, bagel chips, veggies and potato chips. Set an inverted plate or shallow pan under one side of the bottom of each basket to create a tilt...looks so nice and guests can grab dippers easily!

Crispy Parmesan Pita Crackers *Makes 10 servings*

6 pita rounds   grated Parmesan cheese

Split pitas and cut each half into 6 wedges. Arrange on an ungreased baking sheet; spray lightly with non-stick vegetable spray. Sprinkle with grated Parmesan. Bake at 350 degrees for 10 minutes, until crisp.

Fresh Tortilla Chips *Makes 8 servings*

6 flour tortillas   salt

Cut each tortilla into 8 wedges; sprinkle lightly with salt. Place on an ungreased baking sheet. Bake at 350 degrees for 15 minutes, until golden.

Group a selection of appetizers on a small table separate from
the main serving tables...early-comers can nibble while
the rest of the crowd gathers.

Oven-Toasted Potato Chips

Makes 4 to 6 servings

1 lb. redskin potatoes,
    sliced 1/8-inch thick

2 T. olive oil
1/2 t. salt, divided

Rinse potato slices in a colander under very cold water; pat dry.
Toss with oil and 1/4 teaspoon salt; spread in a single layer on
a lightly greased baking sheet. Bake on top oven rack at 500 degrees
for 20 to 25 minutes, until golden. Sprinkle with remaining salt;
serve warm.

Jelly jars make lovely lanterns for backyard gatherings!
Nestle a tea light inside and hang with wire from
tree branches or fenceposts. Look for citronella
candles to keep mosquitoes away.

Sweet Potato Chips

Makes 4 servings

2 sweet potatoes, peeled
   and thinly sliced
1 t. sugar

1 t. salt
1-1/2 T. chili powder
1/4 to 1/2 t. ground cumin

Arrange sweet potato slices on a lightly greased baking sheet; set aside. Combine sugar, salt and spices in a small bowl; sprinkle half of mixture lightly over slices. Bake at 325 degrees for 15 minutes. Turn slices over; sprinkle with remaining sugar mixture. Bake for an additional 15 minutes. Cool on a wire rack.

Easy as A-B-C! Shape dough for Homemade Pretzels into letters...spell out names, "Congrats!" or "Celebrate!"

Homemade Pretzels

Makes one to 2 dozen

1 env. active dry yeast
1-1/2 c. warm water
1 T. sugar
1 t. salt

3 to 4 c. all-purpose flour
1 egg, beaten
Garnish: coarse salt

Dissolve yeast in water; add sugar and salt. Add flour 1/2 cup at a time; mix dough and knead. Roll out into a thin rope and form into pretzel shapes. Place on a greased baking sheet; brush with egg and sprinkle with salt. Bake at 450 degrees for 12 minutes, until golden.

Creamy Mustard Dip

Makes one cup

8-oz. container sour cream
2 t. mustard

1/2 t. onion salt

Stir together ingredients; chill for 30 minutes.

Use any favorite quiche recipe to make mini quiche appetizers.
Just pour ingredients into greased mini muffin cups and bake until
the centers are set...so simple!

Pepperoni Pizza Puffs

Makes 3 dozen

1 c. milk
1 egg, beaten
1 c. all-purpose flour
1 t. baking powder

1 c. shredded pizza-blend
  cheese
1-1/2 c. pepperoni, diced

Whisk together milk and egg; stir in flour, baking powder and cheese. Mix well; fold in pepperoni. Let stand for 15 minutes. Fill lightly greased mini muffin cups 3/4 full. Bake at 350 degrees for 25 to 35 minutes, or until golden.

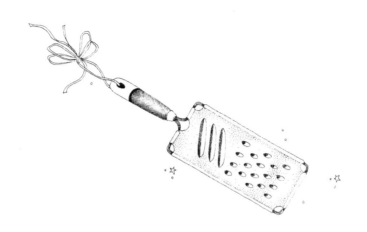

When serving appetizers, a good rule of thumb for quantities
is 6 to 8 per person if dinner will follow and 12 to 15 per person
if it's an appetizer-only gathering.

Golden Cheese Puffs

Makes 3 dozen

8-oz. pkg. cream cheese,
   softened
1/2 c. mayonnaise
1/4 c. grated Parmesan cheese

2 T. onion, chopped
1/8 t. cayenne pepper
1 loaf sliced party rye

Mix together cream cheese, mayonnaise, Parmesan, onion and
cayenne pepper. Spread on bread slices; arrange on ungreased
baking sheets. Bake at 425 degrees until golden and bubbly,
about 15 minutes.

Add a little lemon-lime soda to fruit juice for a fizzy treat
that's refreshing with party foods.

Baja Bites

Makes about 2-1/2 dozen

5 eggs, beaten
8-oz. container cottage cheese
1/4 c. all-purpose flour
1/2 t. baking powder
1/4 c. butter, melted

2 T. green onion, minced
4-oz. can diced green
  chiles, drained
8-oz. pkg. shredded Monterey
  Jack cheese

Combine eggs and cottage cheese; blend until almost smooth.
Add flour, baking powder and butter; stir in onion, chiles and cheese.
Pour into a lightly greased 8"x8" baking pan. Bake at 350 degrees for
30 to 40 minutes. Let cool slightly; cut into squares.

Fill an old-fashioned blue glass canning jar with Zesty Mozzarella Cheese Bites...attach a hand-stamped or printed label. Tuck into a basket with some seasoned crackers. A gift cheese lovers will enjoy!

Zesty Mozzarella Cheese Bites *Makes 14 servings*

16-oz. pkg. mozzarella cheese,
    sliced into 1/2-inch cubes
1/4 c. roasted garlic oil
2 t. balsamic vinegar

2 T. fresh basil, chopped
1 T. mixed whole peppercorns,
    coarsely ground

Place cheese cubes in a medium bowl; set aside. Whisk remaining
ingredients together and pour over cheese cubes. Toss to coat;
cover and refrigerate up to 3 days.

Socials are all about bringing family & friends together,
so scatter disposable cameras on tables and chairs to
encourage lots of picture taking!

Savory Baked Spinach Balls

Makes 10 dozen

3 lbs. spinach, chopped,
   cooked and drained
2 c. herb-flavored stuffing mix
2 onions, minced
5 eggs, beaten
3/4 c. butter, melted

1/2 c. grated Parmesan cheese
2 cloves garlic, minced
1/2 t. salt
1/4 t. pepper
1 t. dried thyme

Combine all ingredients in a large mixing bowl; mix well. Shape
into one-inch balls; arrange on ungreased baking sheets. Bake at
350 degrees for 15 minutes; serve warm.

For stand-up parties, make it easy on guests by serving foods that can be eaten in just one or 2 bites.

"Fried" Mozzarella Sticks

Makes one dozen

2 eggs
1 T. water
1 c. bread crumbs
2-1/2 t. Italian seasoning
1/2 t. garlic powder

1/8 t. pepper
12 string cheese sticks
3 T. all-purpose flour
1 T. butter, melted

Whisk eggs and water together in a small bowl; set aside. Combine crumbs, Italian seasoning, garlic powder and pepper in a plastic zipping bag; set aside. Coat cheese sticks in flour; dip in egg mixture, then shake in crumb mixture. Cover and refrigerate for 4 hours. Arrange on an ungreased baking sheet; drizzle with butter. Bake at 400 degrees for 6 to 8 minutes. Let stand for 3 to 5 minutes before serving.

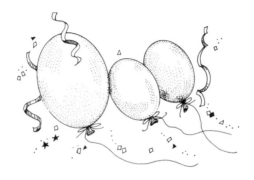

Here's a fun way to invite guests over! Fill bouquets of balloons with helium and write the who, what and where party information on each with a permanent pen. Hand deliver or tie securely to doorknobs with lengths of curling ribbon.

Fiesta Nachos

Makes 12 servings

15-oz. pkg. tortilla chips
1 lb. ground beef, browned
    and drained
1-1/2 c. shredded Cheddar
    cheese
1-1/2 c. shredded Monterey
    Jack cheese

8-oz. container sour cream
2 c. salsa
1 sweet onion, diced
1 bunch green onions, chopped
2 tomatoes, diced
4-oz. can sliced black olives,
    drained

Layer tortilla chips over the bottom of an ungreased 13"x9" baking pan; top with ground beef. Sprinkle with shredded cheeses. Bake at 375 degrees for 10 to 15 minutes, or until cheeses are melted. Remove from oven; layer with sour cream and then salsa. Sprinkle onions, tomatoes and olives over top.

Use pretty glass trifle bowls to hold pillar candles...keep them in place with treats like candy corn, mini pretzels, popcorn or even dried cranberries.

3-Pepper Quesadillas

Makes 2-1/2 dozen

1 green pepper, thinly sliced
1 red pepper, thinly sliced
1 yellow pepper, thinly sliced
1/2 onion, thinly sliced
1/3 c. margarine
1/2 t. ground cumin

8-oz. pkg. cream cheese, softened
1/2 c. grated fresh Parmesan cheese
10 6-inch flour tortillas

In a skillet over medium heat, sauté peppers and onions in margarine until tender; stir in cumin. Drain, reserving drippings. Blend cheeses with an electric mixer on medium speed until well mixed. Spread 2 tablespoons cheese mixture onto each tortilla. Top with pepper mixture; fold tortillas in half and place on an ungreased baking sheet. Brush tops with reserved drippings; bake at 425 degrees for 10 minutes. Slice each tortilla into thirds.

"Stay" is a charming word in a friend's vocabulary.
-Louisa May Alcott

Easy Stromboli Slices

Makes 8 servings

1 loaf frozen bread
    dough, thawed
2 eggs, separated
2 T. oil
1 t. dried oregano
1 t. dried parsley
1/2 t. garlic powder

1/4 t. pepper
4-oz. pkg. sliced pepperoni
8-oz. pkg. shredded mozzarella
    cheese
1 T. grated Parmesan cheese
Garnish: pizza sauce or garlic
    butter, warmed

Roll out bread dough into a 15"x12" rectangle; set aside. Combine egg yolks, oil and seasonings; spread over dough. Arrange pepperoni and mozzarella cheese on top; sprinkle with Parmesan cheese. Roll up; place seam-side down on a lightly greased baking sheet. Lightly beat egg whites and brush over top. Bake at 350 degrees for 30 to 40 minutes. Slice and serve with pizza sauce or garlic butter for dipping.

Have appetizers for dinner! Set up a family-size sampler with pizza snacks, mini egg rolls, potato skins and lots of dippers to try too. Don't forget the French fries!

Pizza Parlor Crescent Snacks *Makes 8 servings*

8-oz. tube refrigerated
   crescent rolls
24 slices pepperoni

2 c. shredded mozzarella cheese
Garnish: 14-oz. jar pizza sauce,
   warmed

Separate rolls into 4 squares; press together seams. Arrange 6 slices pepperoni on each square; top with cheese. Roll tightly lengthwise and slice each roll into 4 pieces. Place on an ungreased baking sheet. Bake at 375 degrees for 12 minutes, or until golden and cheese is bubbling. Serve with pizza sauce for dipping.

Stock up on festive party napkins, candles and table decorations
at post–holiday sales. Tuck them away in a big box...you'll be
all set to turn a casual get-together into a party.

Bubble Pizza

Makes 8 to 10 servings

3 7-1/2 oz. tubes refrigerated
   buttermilk biscuits,
   quartered
14-oz. jar pizza sauce, divided
1 clove garlic, minced

3 c. shredded mozzarella
   cheese, divided
Optional: sliced pepperoni,
   mushrooms, onion, ham,
   sausage or pineapple

Place biscuit pieces in a large mixing bowl; add half the pizza sauce,
garlic and 2 cups cheese. Mix until biscuit pieces are well coated;
spread in a greased 13"x9" baking pan. Pour remaining sauce over
top; add any optional toppings. Sprinkle with remaining cheese. Bake
at 350 degrees for 40 to 45 minutes.

If someone volunteers to pitch in with get-together
preparations, or offers to bring a dish, let them!
Just be sure to return the favor.

Favorite Veggie Pizza

Makes about 1-1/2 dozen

8-oz. tube refrigerated
    crescent rolls
8-oz. pkg. cream cheese,
    softened
1/4 c. sour cream
1/3 c. mayonnaise
1-oz. pkg. ranch salad
    dressing mix

3/4 c. broccoli, chopped
3/4 c. cauliflower, chopped
3/4 c. carrot, chopped
3/4 c. green onion, chopped
3/4 c. green pepper, chopped
3/4 c. tomato, chopped
3/4 c. shredded Cheddar cheese

Spread out rolls to cover the bottom of a greased 13"x9" baking pan; pinch seams together. Bake at 350 degrees for 7 to 8 minutes; set aside to cool. Mix cream cheese, sour cream, mayonnaise and salad dressing mix; spread over crust. Sprinkle with vegetables; top with cheese. Cover with plastic wrap, gently pressing toppings into dressing layer; refrigerate for 3 to 4 hours. Cut into squares to serve.

A 2 or 3-tier pie server becomes a terrific way
to display bite-size appetizers. Just set a plate
of goodies on each tier!

Make-Ahead Ham Bites

Makes one dozen

12 Hawaiian rolls, separated
    and halved
1 lb. sliced cooked ham
1/2 lb. sliced Swiss cheese

3/4 c. butter, melted
1-1/2 t. Dijon mustard
1-1/2 t. Worcestershire sauce
1-1/2 t. dried, minced onion

Arrange bottoms of rolls in an ungreased 13"x9" baking pan; layer ham and cheese on top. Replace tops of rolls. Whisk remaining ingredients together; drizzle evenly over rolls. Cover and refrigerate overnight. Uncover and bake at 350 degrees for 15 to 20 minutes.

Alongside sticky finger foods like chicken wings, set out a basket of rolled-up washcloths, moistened with lemon-scented water and warmed briefly in the microwave. Guests will thank you!

Spicy Honey Chicken Wings *Makes about 2-1/2 dozen*

1/2 c. chili sauce
1 T. soy sauce
1 T. honey

1/2 t. dry mustard
1/4 t. cayenne pepper
2 to 3 lbs. chicken wings

Combine sauces, honey, mustard and cayenne pepper in a lightly greased 3-quart baking dish. Add chicken wings and toss to coat; cover and refrigerate for one hour. Uncover and bake at 350 degrees for 45 to 60 minutes, turning occasionally.

A punch bowl is a festive touch that makes even the simplest party beverage special! Surround it with a simple wreath of fresh flowers or even bunches of grapes.

Oriental Chicken Wings

Makes about 4 dozen

16-oz. bottle soy sauce
1 onion, chopped
1 c. sugar

1 t. ground ginger
5-lb. pkg. frozen chicken wings

Mix together soy sauce, onion, sugar and ginger in a medium bowl.
Arrange frozen chicken wings in 2 ungreased 13"x9" baking pans;
pour mixture over wings. Bake, uncovered, at 350 degrees for
1-1/2 to 2 hours, turning every 20 minutes.

Put out the welcome mat and invite friends over for appetizers...
keep it simple so everyone's free to visit.

Waikiki Meatballs

Makes 2 dozen

1-1/2 lbs. ground beef
2/3 c. cracker crumbs
1/3 c. onion, minced
1 egg, beaten
1/4 c. milk
1-1/2 t. salt
1/4 t. ground ginger

1/2 c. brown sugar, packed
2 T. cornstarch
20-oz. can pineapple chunks,
    drained and juice reserved
1/3 c. vinegar
1 T. soy sauce
1/4 c. green pepper, chopped

Combine ground beef, crumbs, onion, egg, milk, salt and ginger, blending well. Shape into one-inch balls and brown in a lightly greased skillet; drain and set aside. Combine brown sugar and cornstarch in a large saucepan over medium heat; blend in reserved pineapple juice, vinegar and soy sauce. Add pineapple chunks, green pepper and meatballs; simmer until warmed through.

Patio chats can last well into the evening, so set out twinkling votives nestled inside colorful retro drinking glasses. Add some sea salt crystals inside the glasses...they'll steady the votives and add sparkle.

Swedish Meatballs

Makes 2 to 3 dozen

2 lbs. ground beef
1 c. cracker crumbs
2 eggs, beaten
1 t. garlic, minced
1/2 t. salt
1 T. olive oil

10-3/4 oz. can cream of
    mushroom soup
10-3/4 oz. can cream of
    chicken soup
1/2 c. plus 2 T. milk

Combine ground beef, crumbs, eggs, garlic and salt; mix well and shape into one-inch balls. Brown meatballs in olive oil in a skillet; drain. Arrange meatballs in an ungreased 13"x9" baking pan; set aside. Combine soups and milk; blend well and pour over meatballs. Cover and bake at 350 degrees until bubbly, about 25 minutes.

Guests will love nibbling even more when appetizers are served in creative ways...try using a wooden cutting board, mirror, LP record, chessboard or an old-fashioned washboard. Fun!

Crabbies

Makes 4 dozen

6-oz. can crabmeat, drained
5-oz. jar sharp pasteurized
    process cheese spread
1/2 c. butter, softened

1-1/2 t. mayonnaise
1/2 t. salt
1/4 t. garlic powder
6 English muffins, split

Mix together all ingredients except English muffins; spread on muffin halves. Cut muffin halves into quarters; arrange on an ungreased broiler pan. Broil until golden and bubbly, about 5 to 6 minutes.

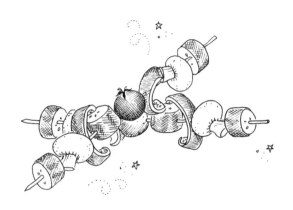

Soak wooden skewers in water for at least 30 minutes
before grilling...they won't burn on the grill.

Grilled Shrimp Skewers

Makes 12 to 15 servings

2 lbs. jumbo shrimp, peeled
    and cleaned
1 c. orange juice
1/4 c. soy sauce
1/4 c. olive oil
1/4 c. sugar

3 cloves garlic, minced
1 T. fresh ginger, peeled
    and minced
1 T. lemon zest
Optional: 1 pt. cherry tomatoes

Place shrimp in a large plastic zipping bag; set aside. Whisk together remaining ingredients in a small bowl and pour over shrimp. Refrigerate for at least one hour, turning occasionally to coat shrimp. Thread shrimp onto short skewers, alternating with cherry tomatoes if desired. Grill over medium coals for about 2 minutes on each side, basting occasionally with marinade.

Look beyond traditional napkins when hosting family & friends.
Try using bandannas, colorful tea towels, inexpensive fabrics
from the craft store or, for especially saucy foods, use
moistened washcloths...they'll love it!

Sesame Beef Strips

Makes 4 servings

6 T. soy sauce
2 T. sugar
1 green onion, sliced
2 cloves garlic, minced
1 T. toasted sesame seed,
    crushed

1 t. fresh ginger, peeled
    and minced
1/8 t. pepper
1-1/2 lbs. beef sirloin, sliced
    into 1/8-inch thick strips

Whisk together all ingredients except beef in a large bowl; add beef, tossing to coat. Cover and refrigerate for 2 hours. Drain, reserving marinade; bring to a boil for use as a dipping sauce. Thread beef strips onto short skewers. Arrange skewers on a broiler pan; broil beef to desired doneness. Serve with reserved marinade.

Add a warm glow to the party with a simple strand of lights.
Decorate the table with a string of white lights folded
inside a sheer table runner or strip of fabric. Sparkly!

Ham & Pineapple Kabobs

Makes 8 to 12 servings

1-1/2 lbs. smoked ham, cubed
8-oz. can pineapple chunks,
   drained and juice reserved

2 T. soy sauce
2 T. brown sugar, packed
1/8 t. ground ginger

Thread ham and pineapple chunks alternately onto short skewers; place in a 2-quart casserole dish. Combine reserved juice with soy sauce, brown sugar and ginger; pour over kabobs, turning to coat. Cover and refrigerate for 2 hours, turning occasionally. Grill over medium coals, turning twice and brushing with marinade, until hot and golden, about 10 minutes.

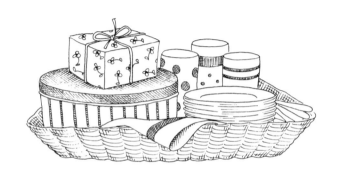

Appetizer parties are a great way to visit during the busy
holiday season. The recipes are so quick & easy to prepare
that more time can be spent catching up!

Coconut Chicken

Makes 4 to 6 servings

1/2 c. milk
3 eggs
3/4 c. all-purpose flour
7-oz. pkg. sweetened flaked
    coconut

salt and pepper to taste
2 to 3 boneless, skinless
    chicken breasts, cubed
oil for deep frying

Whisk milk and eggs together; add flour and whisk until smooth.
Add coconut, salt and pepper; dip chicken in mixture. Heat one-inch
depth oil to 365 degrees in a deep skillet. Add chicken a few pieces at
a time; deep-fry until golden on both sides and juices run clear when
pierced with a fork, about 15 minutes. Drain on paper towels.

Keep 'em cold! Fill a large galvanized tub with ice, then nestle bottles of soda or lemonade in the ice to keep chilled. Everyone can help themselves!

Spicy Buffalo Bites

Makes 3 dozen

3/4 c. cooked chicken, shredded
2 T. Dijon mustard
4 t. hot pepper sauce
36 herb-flavored shredded
    wheat crackers

2 T. margarine, melted
4-oz. pkg. crumbled blue cheese
2 T. celery, minced

Combine chicken, mustard and hot pepper sauce; mix well. Place
one teaspoon mixture on each cracker; drizzle with margarine.
Stir blue cheese and celery together; spread over chicken mixture.
Arrange crackers on ungreased baking sheets; bake at 400 degrees
until cheese melts, about 4 minutes.

Share silly memories at the next get-together of
friends & family. Ask everyone to jot down their favorites
and toss them in a hat. Pull them out one at a time
to read out loud...guaranteed giggles!

Sausage Stars

Makes about 2 dozen

25-count pkg. wonton wrappers
1 lb. ground sausage, browned
    and drained
1-1/2 c. shredded sharp
    Cheddar cheese
1-1/2 c. shredded Monterey
    Jack cheese

1 c. ranch salad dressing
2-1/4 oz. can sliced black
    olives, drained
1/2 c. red pepper, chopped

Press wonton wrappers into lightly greased muffin cups; bake at 350 degrees for 5 minutes. Remove wontons and place on an ungreased baking sheet. Combine remaining ingredients; mix well and spoon into baked wontons. Bake at 350 degrees for 5 minutes, or until bubbly.

Quickly dress up a table by filling a glass bowl with seasonal
objects...pine cones and ornaments during winter, dyed eggs in
spring, seashells in summer and shiny apples during fall.

Quick Mini Sausage Wraps

Makes 2-1/2 dozen

3 10-oz. pkgs. mini smoked
   sausages

1 lb. bacon, sliced into thirds
1/2 c. brown sugar, packed

Wrap each sausage with a bacon slice; secure with a toothpick.
Place in an ungreased 13"x9" baking pan; sprinkle with brown sugar.
Bake at 350 degrees for about one hour. Drain on paper towels.

Mini Pigs in Blankets

Makes 4 dozen

2 8-oz. tubes refrigerated
   crescent rolls

16-oz. pkg. mini smoked
   sausages

Separate rolls into 4 rectangles; roll out 1/8-inch thick. Slice each into
6 strips; roll a sausage in each strip. Arrange on an ungreased baking
sheet. Bake at 375 degrees for 10 to 12 minutes, until golden.

If you need extra chairs for a get-together, search
flea markets ahead of time for old metal lawn chairs
like Grandma had in her backyard. Just give them
a face lift with a new coat of paint.

Favorite Sausage Balls

Makes about 5 dozen

1 lb. ground sausage
2 c. biscuit baking mix

12-oz. pkg. shredded Cheddar
  cheese

Combine ingredients and mix well; shape into one-inch balls.
Arrange on ungreased baking sheets; bake at 425 degrees for
12 to 15 minutes.

A true friend is the best possession.

-Benjamin Franklin

Cherry Tomato Poppers

Makes 2 to 3 dozen

2 pts. cherry tomatoes
1 lb. bacon, crisply cooked and
    crumbled

1/2 c. mayonnaise
1/2 c. onion, minced
3 T. shredded mozzarella cheese

Use a small spoon or knife tip to hollow out tomatoes; invert and
drain on paper towels. Combine remaining ingredients; spoon into
centers of tomatoes. Chill until serving time.

Line baking sheets with parchment paper cut to fit...there's
no sticking and clean-up is oh-so easy.

Italian Eggplant Sticks

Makes 10 to 12 servings

3 eggplants, peeled
1 c. Italian seasoned dry
    bread crumbs
1 t. salt
1 t. pepper

3 eggs
1/4 c. milk
oil for deep frying
Garnish: salsa, sour cream or
    warmed marinara sauce

Slice eggplants into 3"x1/2" sticks; place in ice water for 30 minutes.
Drain and set aside. Combine bread crumbs, salt and pepper in a
shallow bowl; set aside. Whisk eggs and milk together in another
shallow bowl. Dip eggplant sticks into egg mixture; coat with
crumbs. Arrange on an ungreased baking sheet; cover and chill for
30 minutes. Heat oil one-inch deep to 365 degrees in a deep skillet.
Add eggplant sticks a few at a time; deep-fry until golden on both
sides, about 2 minutes. Drain on paper towels. Serve with dipping
sauces as desired.

Mini choppers make prep work a breeze for chopping mushrooms,
onions, tomatoes or peppers...what a time-saver!

Cheesy Bacon Mushrooms

Makes 2 to 3 dozen

16-oz. pkg. mushrooms, stems
    removed and finely chopped
1 onion, chopped
1/4 c. margarine

1 c. shredded mozzarella cheese
3-oz. jar bacon bits
1/2 to 1 c. dry bread crumbs

In a skillet over medium heat, sauté mushroom stems and onion
in margarine until tender. Remove from heat; stir in cheese, bacon
bits and crumbs, mixing well. Spoon mixture into mushroom caps;
place in an ungreased 13"x9" baking pan. Bake at 350 degrees for
12 to 15 minutes, or until golden.

Curl a string of dried chile peppers into a circle, then set a hurricane with a plump red candle in the center for a quick and casual centerpiece.

Sausage-Stuffed Mushrooms   *Makes 2 to 3 dozen*

1/2 lb. ground sausage
16-oz. pkg. mushrooms, stems
    removed and finely chopped
1/4 c. onion, chopped

1/3 c. catsup
2 T. dry bread crumbs
1 t. dried parsley
1/2 t. dried basil

Cook sausage, mushroom stems and onion in a large skillet over
medium heat until sausage is browned. Remove from heat; drain.
Stir in catsup, crumbs, parsley and basil. Fill mushroom caps with
mixture; place in an ungreased 13"x9" baking pan. Bake at
375 degrees for 12 to 15 minutes, or until golden.

Great for a kids' party...serve finger foods on
a plastic flying disc for each child. What fun!

Cheddar Potato Skins

Makes 2 dozen

6 baking potatoes
1 c. finely shredded Cheddar
   cheese

2 T. green onion, finely chopped
1/8 t. garlic powder
Garnish: sour cream, salsa

Bake potatoes at 425 degrees for 40 to 50 minutes, until tender.
Quarter each potato lengthwise and scoop out insides, leaving
1/2-inch thick shells. Arrange potato shells skin-side up on an
ungreased baking sheet; spray skins evenly with non-stick vegetable
spray. Bake, uncovered, at 425 degrees for 20 to 25 minutes, until
crisp. Turn shells skin-side down. Toss together cheese, onion and
garlic powder; sprinkle evenly over shells. Return to oven for an
additional 2 minutes, until cheese melts. Serve with sour cream
and salsa.

Colorful straws layered with slices of kiwi, banana, strawberries and pineapple are fun fruit skewers for glasses of sparkling soda or frosty lemonade!

Stuffed Jalapeños

Makes 3 dozen

8-oz. pkg. cream cheese, softened
1 c. shredded Cheddar cheese
1 c. mayonnaise
1 clove garlic, minced

18 jalapeños, halved and seeded
1 egg white
1 T. milk
1 c. corn flake cereal, crushed

Mix cheeses, mayonnaise and garlic together; spoon into jalapeño halves. Set aside. Whisk egg white and milk in a shallow bowl; place crushed cereal in another shallow bowl. Dip each jalapeño into egg white mixture and roll in cereal to coat. Arrange on an ungreased baking sheet; bake at 375 degrees for 15 minutes.

Start a kitchen journal to note favorite recipes, family
preferences, even special dinner guests and celebrations.
It'll make planning meals and parties much easier and later
will become a cherished keepsake.

Fried Dill Pickles

Makes 12 servings

32-oz. jar whole dill pickles,
    drained and sliced
    1/4-inch thick
1 c. milk
1 egg
1 T. Worcestershire sauce
6 drops hot pepper sauce

3-1/2 c. plus 1 T. all-purpose
    flour, divided
3/4 t. salt
3/4 t. pepper
oil for deep frying
Optional: ranch salad dressing

Drain pickle slices on paper towels. Whisk together milk, egg, sauces
and one tablespoon flour in a medium bowl. Mix remaining flour, salt
and pepper in another bowl. Dip pickles into milk mixture, then into
flour mixture. Heat one-inch depth oil to 350 degrees in a deep skillet.
Add pickles a few at a time; deep-fry until golden on both sides. Drain
on paper towels. Serve hot with salad dressing for dipping, if desired.

Decorate plain paper cups with ribbons, bows, stickers and flowers...anything but plain!

Tortilla Roll-Ups

Makes 4 to 5 dozen

8-oz. pkg. cream cheese,
   softened
8-oz. container sour cream
1 onion, chopped
1-1/4 oz. pkg. taco
   seasoning mix
4-oz. can diced green chiles

2 tomatoes, chopped
8-oz. pkg. shredded Cheddar
   cheese
hot pepper sauce to taste
8 to 10 flour tortillas
Garnish: salsa, guacamole

Combine cream cheese, sour cream, onion and seasoning mix until smooth. Stir in chiles, tomatoes, shredded cheese and sauce, blending well. Spread mixture on tortillas; roll up tortillas. Lay seam-side down in an ungreased 13"x9" baking pan; chill until firm. Cut into one-inch slices; fasten with toothpicks. Serve with salsa and guacamole.

Make 2 batches of Savory Ranch Snack Mix and wrap 'em up
in brightly colored cellophane bags to send home with
each guest...a double delight!

Savory Ranch Snack Mix

Makes 6 cups

1 c. canola oil
1-oz. pkg. ranch salad
    dressing mix
1 t. dill weed
1 t. garlic powder

2 c. mini shredded wheat
    squares
2 c. mini pretzels
1 c. peanuts or mixed nuts
1 c. sunflower kernels

Combine oil, dressing mix and seasonings in a small bowl; set aside.
Mix remaining ingredients in a large bowl; pour oil mixture over all
and stir to coat well. Spread on an ungreased 13"x9" baking pan.
Bake at 250 degrees for 15 to 20 minutes, stirring once. Let cool;
store in an airtight container.

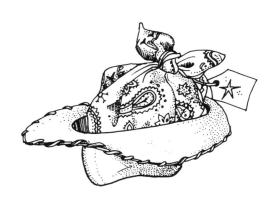

Wrap up Spicy Tex-Mex Mix in a bandanna and
tuck into a cowboy hat...perfect for a backyard BBQ!

Spicy Tex-Mex Mix

Makes 11 cups

3 c. corn chips
3 c. mini shredded wheat cereal
2-1/2 c. mini pretzel squares
2-1/2 c. peanuts

1-1/4 oz. pkg. taco
   seasoning mix
1/4 c. butter, melted

Combine all ingredients in a large bowl; toss well to mix. Store in an airtight container.

Fill a vintage metal picnic basket with Honey-Glazed Snack Mix, add a scoop and place paper bags nearby. Invite everyone to just help themselves to this sweet, crunchy snack mix.

Honey-Glazed Snack Mix

Makes 6-1/2 cups

4 c. bite-size crispy corn
    or wheat cereal squares
1-1/2 c. mini pretzels

1 c. pecan halves
1/3 c. margarine
1/4 c. honey

Combine cereal, pretzels and pecans in a large bowl; set aside.
Melt margarine and honey in a small saucepan over low heat;
pour over mix. Toss to coat; spread on an ungreased baking sheet.
Bake at 350 degrees for 15 minutes. Spread on wax paper to cool.
Store in an airtight container.

A quick & easy sampler of snacks! Place several paper muffin liners, side by side, in a large muffin tin...fill each with a different treat. Try a sampler including a sweet mix with candy, seasoned nuts and a hearty trail mix...yum!

Barbecue Pecans

Makes 4 cups

4 c. pecan halves
1/2 c. butter, melted
2 T. Worcestershire sauce
2 t. seasoned salt
1 t. barbecue sauce

1 t. smoke-flavored cooking
   sauce
1/2 t. hot pepper sauce
Optional: 1 t. flavor enhancer

Place pecans in an ungreased 13"x9" baking pan; set aside. Mix remaining ingredients together in a small bowl; drizzle over nuts, tossing to coat. Spread pecans evenly in pan. Bake at 300 degrees for 25 to 30 minutes, stirring every 8 to 10 minutes. Let cool; store in an airtight container.

For lasting memories, keep a scrapbook of every celebration.
Fill it with invitations, photos, pressed flowers...anything
that's a sweet reminder. Be sure to leave room for
handwritten notes too.

Cinnamon & Ginger Nuts

Makes 3 cups

3 c. mixed nuts
1 egg white
1 T. orange juice
2/3 c. sugar

1 t. cinnamon
1/2 t. ground ginger
1/2 t. allspice

Place nuts in a large bowl; set aside. Blend egg white and orange juice together until frothy; stir in sugar and spices. Pour over nuts; mix thoroughly. Spread nuts on an aluminum foil-lined baking sheet. Bake at 275 degrees for 45 minutes, stirring every 15 minutes. Let cool; store in an airtight container.

Ask the local pizza parlor for a new pizza box...wrap up a
Brownie-Nut Pizza as a gift for a lucky college student!

Brownie-Nut Pizza

Makes 10 to 12 servings

2 21-oz. pkgs. brownie mix
2 8-oz. pkgs. cream cheese,
  softened
1/2 c. creamy peanut butter
1/2 c. sugar
2 t. vanilla extract

6-oz. pkg. semi-sweet chocolate
  chips, divided
1/2 c. chopped walnuts
1/2 c. peanut butter chips
1 T. butter
1 T. milk

Prepare brownie mixes according to package directions; spread on a greased 16" round pizza pan. Bake at 350 degrees for 15 minutes, or until a toothpick inserted in center tests clean; cool. Combine cream cheese, peanut butter, sugar and vanilla; spread over brownie. Sprinkle 1/2 cup chocolate chips, nuts and peanut butter chips over top. Melt together remaining chocolate chips, butter and milk; drizzle over top. Chill for one hour; cut into wedges to serve.

Short on time and need a festive dessert fast? Dip plump strawberries or mandarin orange slices into melted semi-sweet chocolate. Set on wax paper and chill until chocolate is firm, then arrange on a paper doily-covered tray.

Caramel Apple Cookie Pizza

Makes 8 to 10 servings

2 apples, cored, peeled
    and sliced
1 to 2 t. lemon juice
18-oz. tube refrigerated sugar
    cookie dough

8-oz. pkg. cream cheese,
    softened
1/2 c. creamy peanut butter
6-oz. jar caramel topping
1/4 c. chopped nuts

Toss apple slices with lemon juice to prevent browning; set aside.
Press cookie dough into an ungreased 12" round pizza pan; bake
according to package directions. Cool. Combine cream cheese and
peanut butter; spread over cooled crust. Arrange apple slices on top;
drizzle with caramel topping and sprinkle with nuts. Cut into wedges
to serve.

Brown bag it! Crinkle brown paper lunch bags and roll down the tops. Fill bags with assorted nuts and snacks...quick, easy and no clean-up!

Chocolate Chip Cheese Ball

Makes 2 cups

8-oz. pkg. cream cheese,
    softened
1/2 c. butter, softened
1/4 t. vanilla extract
3/4 c. powdered sugar
2 T. brown sugar, packed

3/4 c. mini semi-sweet
    chocolate chips
3/4 c. chopped pecans
vanilla wafers or mini
    sugar cookies

Combine cream cheese, butter and vanilla; blend until fluffy. Add sugars; mix well. Fold in chocolate chips; cover and refrigerate for 2 hours. Shape into a ball; cover with plastic wrap and refrigerate for an additional hour. At serving time, unwrap and roll in pecans. Serve with wafers or small cookies for dipping.

New neighbor on the block? Surprise them with a basket
of fresh fruit along with a crock full of this
Marshmallow Fruit Dip...they'll love it!

Marshmallow Fruit Dip

Makes 2 cups

8-oz. pkg. cream cheese,
  softened
3 T. frozen orange juice
  concentrate, thawed

7-oz. jar marshmallow creme
apple, pear and banana slices

Blend cream cheese and orange juice together until smooth; stir in
marshmallow creme. Refrigerate until well chilled. Serve with fruit
slices for dipping.

Dress up a dessert tray in no time for a grand ending to your party! Place Mocha Truffles in bright red or gold foil candy cups.

Mocha Truffles

Makes 5 to 6 dozen

2 12-oz. pkgs. semi-sweet
  chocolate chips
8-oz. pkg. cream cheese,
  softened

3 T. instant coffee granules
2 t. water
16-oz. pkg. dark chocolate
  melting chocolate, chopped

Place chocolate chips in a microwave-safe bowl. Microwave on high
setting at 30-second intervals until melted; stir until smooth. Add
cream cheese, coffee granules and water; mix well with an electric
mixer on medium setting. Chill until firm enough to shape; form into
one-inch balls and place on wax paper-lined baking sheets. Chill for
an additional one to 2 hours, until firm. Place melting chocolate in a
microwave-safe bowl; melt as for chocolate chips. Use a small fork or
dipping tool to dip balls in melted chocolate. Return to wax paper-lined
baking sheets to set.

Someone's sure to ask, so jot down your recipe on a copy of our handy recipe card. And if you write the recipe name on a table tent, everyone will know what you've brought! Just copy, cut, fold in half and set alongside your dish.

Sweet Red Pepper Dip

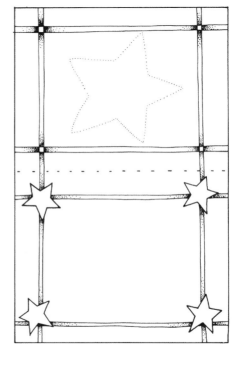

from the kitchen of : _____

_____

_____

_____

_____

_____

_____

_____

Copy this recipe card...share your favorite
appetizer recipe with a friend!

INDEX

BITE-SIZE SNACKS

Baja Bites	41
"Fried" Mozzarella Sticks	47
Golden Cheese Puffs	39
Pepperoni Pizza Puffs	37
Savory Baked Spinach Balls	45
Zesty Mozzarella Cheese Bites	43

CHIPS & DIPPERS

Crispy Parmesan Pita Crackers	29
Fresh Tortilla Chips	29
Homemade Pretzels	35
Oven-Toasted Potato Chips	31
Sweet Potato Chips	33

DESSERT TREATS

Brownie-Nut Pizza	115
Caramel Apple Cookie Pizza	117
Chocolate Chip Cheese Ball	119
Marshmallow Fruit Dip	121
Mocha Truffles	123

DIPS & SPREADS

Always-Requested Spinach Dip	19
Cool & Creamy Mexican Dip	7
Creamy Mustard Dip	35
Delicious Chile-Corn Dip	5
Dried Beef & Cheese Ball	27
Garden-Fresh Veggie Dip	21
Homemade Guacamole	9
Oh-So-Good Artichoke Dip	15
Scrumptious Bacon-Cheese Dip	3
Seashore Crab Spread	23
Sweet Red Pepper Dip	17
Touchdown Hot Taco Dip	13
Yummy Chicken-Salsa Dip	11
Zippy Cheese Ball	25

MEATY TREATS

Coconut Chicken	79
Crabbies	71
Favorite Sausage Balls	87
Grilled Shrimp Skewers	73
Ham & Pineapple Kabobs	77
Make-Ahead Ham Bites	61

INDEX

Mini Pigs in Blankets   85
Oriental Chicken Wings   65
Quick Mini Sausage Wraps   85
Sausage Stars   83
Sesame Beef Strips   75
Spicy Buffalo Bites   81
Spicy Honey Chicken Wings   63
Swedish Meatballs   69
Waikiki Meatballs   67

NUTS & SNACK MIXES
Barbecue Pecans   111
Cinnamon & Ginger Nuts   113
Honey-Glazed Snack Mix   109
Savory Ranch Snack Mix   105
Spicy Tex-Mex Mix   107

PIZZA & TORTILLA SNACKS
3-Pepper Quesadillas   51
Bubble Pizza   57
Easy Stromboli Slices   53

Favorite Veggie Pizza   59
Fiesta Nachos   49
Pizza Parlor Crescent Snacks   55

VEGGIE BITES
Cheddar Potato Skins   97
Cheesy Bacon Mushrooms   93
Cherry Tomato Poppers   89
Fried Dill Pickles   101
Italian Eggplant Sticks   91
Sausage-Stuffed Mushrooms   95
Stuffed Jalapeños   99
Tortilla Roll-Ups   103

Our Story

Back in 1984, we were next-door neighbors raising our families in the little town of Delaware, Ohio. Two moms with small children, we were looking for a way to do what we loved and stay home with the kids too. We had always shared a love of home cooking and making memories with family & friends and so, after many a conversation over the backyard fence, **Gooseberry Patch** was born.

We put together our first catalog at our kitchen tables, enlisting the help of our loved ones wherever we could. From that very first mailing, we found an immediate connection with many of our customers and it wasn't long before we began receiving letters, photos and recipes from these new friends. In 1992, we put together our very first cookbook, compiled from hundreds of these recipes and, the rest, as they say, is history.

Hard to believe it's been over 30 years since those kitchen-table days! From that original little **Gooseberry Patch** family, we've grown to include an amazing group of creative folks who love cooking, decorating and creating as much as we do. Today, we're best known for our homestyle, family-friendly cookbooks, now recognized as national bestsellers.

One thing's for sure, we couldn't have done it without our friends all across the country. Each year, we're honored to turn thousands of your recipes into our collectible cookbooks. Our hope is that each book captures the stories and heart of all of you who have shared with us. Whether you've been with us since the beginning or are just discovering us, welcome to the **Gooseberry Patch** family!

Want to hear the latest from **Gooseberry Patch**?
www.gooseberrypatch.com

Vickie & Jo Ann

1•800•854•6673